R.S.C. STRATFORD-on-Avon.

HENRY V

Jo and D

Songs from Shakespeare

For J.M.

WILLIAM SHAKESPEARE
1564-1616

First published 1992 by Walker Books Ltd
87 Vauxhall Walk, London SE11 5HJ

This edition © 1992 Walker Books Ltd
Illustrations © 1992 Louise Brierley

First printed 1992
Printed and bound by South China Printing Co. (1988) Ltd

British Library Cataloguing-in-Publication Data
A catalogue record for this book is available from the British Library.

ISBN 0-7445-1921-7

Songs from Shakespeare

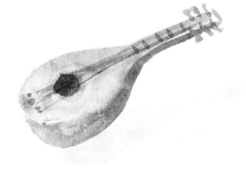

illustrated by Louise Brierley

WALKER BOOKS
LONDON

CONTENTS

INTRODUCTION

UNLIKE his sonnets and other poetry, Shakespeare's songs seem to have attracted very little attention. Few appear in print at all, except in editions of the plays of which they are a part, and I know of no illustrated collection other than this. Yet these songs are among the most wonderful lyrics in the English language, full of rich imagery that nourishes the imagination and exalts the spirit.

On the whole, Shakespeare's songs enhance the mood of his plays, whether they are an integral part – as are Ophelia's lamentations – or an interlude, such as that provided by the songs in *Twelfth Night*. In my illustrations, I have tried to echo and reflect those pervading moods: from the magical beauty of *The Tempest*'s "Full fathom five thy father lies…" to the romantic exuberance of "It was a lover and his lass…" in *As You Like It*; from the Clown's doleful grave-side manner in *Hamlet* to the light-hearted dialogue between Spring and Winter that ends *Love's Labour's Lost*.

My selection is, of course, a very personal one. I have chosen those songs that stir a special emotion in me and which conjure a vivid image in my mind. All of them have given me immense pleasure in one way or another. I hope readers will find equal pleasure in this collection and that they may forgive me if I have omitted any of their favourites.

Corinne Bradley

THE TEMPEST

Ariel: Come unto these yellow sands,
    And then take hands;
Curtsied when you have and kiss'd,
    The wild waves whist,
Foot it featly here and there,
And, sweet sprites, the burden bear.
    Hark, hark!
    Bow-wow.
    The watch dogs bark.
    Bow-wow.
    Hark, hark! I hear
The strain of strutting Chanticleer.
Cry – Cock-a-diddle-dow.

THE TEMPEST

Ariel: Full fathom five thy father lies;
          Of his bones are coral made;
        Those are pearls that were his eyes;
          Nothing of him that doth fade
        But doth suffer a sea-change
        Into something rich and strange.
        Sea-nymphs hourly ring his knell:
          Ding-dong.
        Hark! now I hear them – Ding-dong bell.

The Tempest

Stephano: The master, the swabber, the boatswain, and I,
The gunner, and his mate,
Lov'd Mall, Meg, and Marian, and Margery,
But none of us cared for Kate;
For she had a tongue with a tang,
Would cry to a sailor, "Go, hang!"
She lov'd not the savour of tar nor of pitch,
Yet a tailor might scratch her where'er
she did itch.
Then to sea, boys, and let her go hang!

Caliban: No more dams I'll make for fish;
        Nor fetch in firing
        At requiring,
      Nor scrape trenchering, nor wash dish.
        'Ban 'Ban, Ca-Caliban,
        Has a new master – get a new man.

THE TEMPEST

Ariel: Where the bee sucks, there suck I;
         In a cowslip's bell I lie;
         There I couch when owls do cry.
         On the bat's back I do fly
         After summer merrily.
         Merrily, merrily shall I live now
         Under the blossom that hangs on the bough.

KING LEAR

Edgar: Swithold footed thrice the 'old;
He met the nightmare and her nine-fold;
Bid her alight
And her troth plight,
And aroint thee, witch, aroint thee!

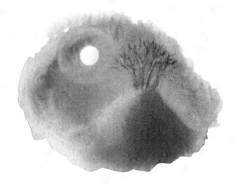

THE MERRY WIVES OF WINDSOR

Sir Hugh Evans: To shallow rivers, to whose falls
Melodious birds sing madrigals;
There will we make our peds of roses,
And a thousand fragrant posies.
To shallow –

Melodious birds sing madrigals –
Whenas I sat in Pabylon –
And a thousand vagram posies.
To shallow *etc.*

The Merry Wives of Windsor

Fairies: Fie on sinful fantasy!
Fie on lust and luxury!
Lust is but a bloody fire,
Kindled with unchaste desire,
Fed in heart, whose flames aspire,
As thoughts do blow them, higher and higher.
Pinch him, fairies, mutually;
Pinch him for his villainy;
Pinch him and burn him and turn him about,
Till candles and star-light and moonshine be out.

Hamlet, Prince of Denmark

Ophelia: Tomorrow is Saint Valentine's day,
        All in the morning betime,
    And I a maid at your window,
        To be your Valentine.

    Then up he rose, and donn'd his clothes,
        And dupp'd the chamber-door;
    Let in the maid, that out a maid
        Never departed more.

    By Gis and by Saint Charity
        Alack, and fie for shame!
    Young men will do't, if they come to't;
        By Cock, they are to blame.
    Quoth she, "Before you tumbled me,
        You promis'd me to wed."
  "So would I 'a done, by yonder sun,
        An thou hadst not come to my bed."

Ophelia: And will 'a not come again?
And will 'a not come again?
No, no, he is dead,
Go to thy death-bed,
He never will come again.

His beard was as white as snow,
All flaxen was his poll;
He is gone, he is gone,
And we cast away moan:
God-a-mercy on his soul!

Hamlet, Prince of Denmark

First Clown: In youth, when I did love, did love,
         Methought it was very sweet,
      To contract-o-the time, for-a my behove,
         O, methought there-a-was nothing-a meet.

      But age, with his stealing steps,
         Hath clawed me in his clutch,
      And hath shipped me intil the land,
         As if I had never been such.

      A pick-axe, and a spade, a spade,
         For and a shrouding sheet;
      O, a pit of clay for to be made
         For such a guest is meet.

LOVE'S LABOUR'S LOST

Spring: When daisies pied and violets blue
And lady-smocks all silver-white
And cuckoo-buds of yellow hue
Do paint the meadows with delight,
The cuckoo then on every tree
Mocks married men; for thus sings he: "Cuckoo;
Cuckoo, cuckoo" – O word of fear,
Unpleasing to a married ear!

When shepherds pipe on oaten straws,
And merry larks are ploughmen's clocks;
When turtles tread, and rooks, and daws,
And maidens bleach their summer smocks;
The cuckoo then on every tree
Mocks married men, for thus sings he: "Cuckoo;
Cuckoo, cuckoo" – O word of fear,
Unpleasing to a married ear!

LOVE'S LABOUR'S LOST

Winter: When icicles hang by the wall,
And Dick the shepherd blows his nail,
And Tom bears logs into the hall,
And milk comes frozen home in pail,
When blood is nipp'd, and ways be foul,
Then nightly sings the staring owl: "Tu-who;
Tu-whit, tu-who" – A merry note,
While greasy Joan doth keel the pot.

When all aloud the wind doth blow,
And coughing drowns the parson's saw,
And birds sit brooding in the snow,
And Marian's nose looks red and raw,
When roasted crabs hiss in the bowl,
Then nightly sings the staring owl: "Tu-who;
Tu-whit, tu-who" – A merry note,
While greasy Joan doth keel the pot.

The Winter's Tale

Autolycus: When daffodils begin to peer,
  With heigh! the doxy over the dale,
Why, then comes in the sweet o' the year,
  For the red blood reigns in the winter's pale.

The white sheet bleaching on the hedge,
  With heigh! the sweet birds, O, how they sing!
Doth set my pugging tooth on edge,
  For a quart of ale is a dish for a king.

The lark, that tirra-lirra chants,
  With heigh! with heigh! the thrush and the jay,
Are summer songs for me and my aunts,
  While we lie tumbling in the hay.

But shall I go mourn for that, my dear?
  The pale moon shines by night;
And when I wander here and there,
  I then do most go right.

If tinkers may have leave to live,
  And bear the sow-skin budget,
Then my account I well may give
  And in the stocks avouch it.

Autolycus: Lawn as white as driven snow;
            Cypress black as e'er was crow;
            Gloves as sweet as damask roses;
            Masks for faces and for noses;
            Bugle bracelet, necklace amber,
            Perfume for a lady's chamber;
            Golden quoifs and stomachers,
            For my lads to give their dears;
            Pins and poking-sticks of steel –
            What maids lack from head to heel.
            Come, buy of me, come; come buy, come buy;
            Buy, lads, or else your lasses cry.
            Come, buy.

THE WINTER'S TALE

Autolycus: Will you buy any tape,
Or lace for your cape,
My dainty duck, my dear-a?
Any silk, any thread,
Any toys for your head,
Of the new'st and fin'st, fin'st wear-a?
Come to the pedlar;
Money's a meddler
That doth utter all men's ware-a.

CYMBELINE

Musicians: Hark, hark! the lark at heaven's gate sings,
      And Phoebus 'gins arise,
His steeds to water at those springs
      On chalic'd flow'rs that lies;
And winking Mary-buds begin
      To ope their golden eyes.
With everything that pretty bin,
      My lady sweet, arise;
      Arise, arise!

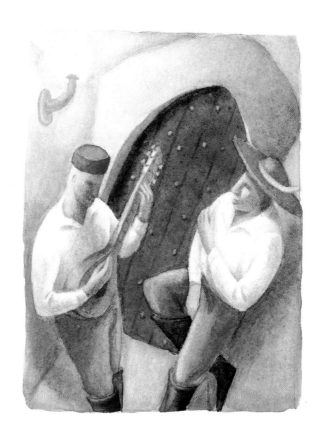

CYMBELINE

Guiderius: Fear no more the heat o' th' sun
    Nor the furious winter's rages;
  Thou thy worldly task hast done,
    Home art gone, and ta'en thy wages.
  Golden lads and girls all must,
  As chimney-sweepers, come to dust.

Arviragus: Fear no more the frown o' th' great;
    Thou art past the tyrant's stroke.
  Care no more to clothe and eat;
    To thee the reed is as the oak.
  The sceptre, learning, physic, must
  All follow this and come to dust.

A Midsummer Night's Dream

First Fairy: You spotted snakes with double tongue,
Thorny hedgehogs, be not seen;
Newts and blind-worms, do no wrong,
Come not near our Fairy Queen.

Chorus: Philomel with melody
Sing in our sweet lullaby.
Lulla, lulla, lullaby; lulla, lulla, lullaby.
   Never harm
   Nor spell nor charm
   Come our lovely lady nigh.
   So good night, with lullaby.

A Midsummer Night's Dream

Bottom: The ousel cock, so black of hue,
  With orange-tawny bill,
The throstle with his note so true,
  The wren with little quill.

The finch, the sparrow, and the lark,
  The plain-song cuckoo grey,
Whose note full many a man doth mark,
  And dares not answer nay —

TWELFTH NIGHT;
OR, WHAT YOU WILL

Clown: O mistress mine, where are you roaming?
O, stay and hear; your true love's coming,
   That can sing both high and low.
Trip no further, pretty sweeting;
Journeys end in lovers meeting,
   Every wise man's son doth know.

What is love? 'Tis not hereafter;
Present mirth hath present laughter;
   What's to come is still unsure.
In delay there lies no plenty,
Then come kiss me, sweet and twenty;
   Youth's a stuff will not endure.

Twelfth Night; or, What You Will

Clown: Come away, come away, death;
      And in sad cypress let me be laid;
    Fly away, fly away, breath,
      I am slain by a fair cruel maid.
    My shroud of white, stuck all with yew,
      O, prepare it!
    My part of death, no one so true
      Did share it.

    Not a flower, not a flower sweet,
      On my black coffin let there be strown;
    Not a friend, not a friend greet
      My poor corpse where my bones shall
      be thrown;
    A thousand thousand sighs to save,
      Lay me, O, where
    Sad true lover never find my grave,
      To weep there!

Clown: When that I was and a little tiny boy,
  With hey, ho, the wind and the rain,
A foolish thing was but a toy,
  For the rain it raineth every day.

But when I came to man's estate,
  With hey, ho, the wind and the rain,
'Gainst knaves and thieves men shut their gate,
  For the rain it raineth every day.

But when I came, alas! to wive,
  With hey, ho, the wind and the rain,
By swaggering could I never thrive,
  For the rain it raineth every day.

But when I came unto my beds,
  With hey, ho, the wind and the rain,
With toss-pots still had drunken heads,
  For the rain it raineth every day.

A great while ago the world begun,
  With hey, ho, the wind and the rain,
But that's all one, our play is done,
  And we'll strive to please you every day.

finis

Othello,
The Moor of Venice

Iago: King Stephen was and a worthy peer,
        His breeches cost him but a crown;
     He held 'em sixpence all too dear,
        With that he call'd the tailor lown.
     He was a wight of high renown,
        And thou art but of low degree.
     'Tis pride that pulls the country down;
        Then take thine auld cloak about thee.

Othello, the Moor of Venice

Desdemona: The poor soul sat sighing by a sycamore tree,
     Sing all a green willow;
Her hand on her bosom, her head on her knee.
     Sing willow, willow, willow.
The fresh streams ran by her, and murmur'd her moans;
     Sing willow, willow, willow;
Her salt tears fell from her and soft'ned the stones;

     Sing willow, willow, willow –

Sing all a green willow must be my garland.
Let nobody blame him; his scorn I approve –

I call'd my love false love; but what said he then?
     Sing willow, willow, willow:
If I court moe women, you'll couch with moe men.

KING HENRY THE EIGHTH

Gentlewoman: Orpheus with his lute made trees,
And the mountain tops that freeze,
  Bow themselves when he did sing;
To his music plants and flowers
Ever sprung, as sun and showers
  There had made a lasting spring.

Every thing that heard him play,
Even the billows of the sea,
  Hung their heads and then lay by.
In sweet music is such art,
Killing care and grief of heart
  Fall asleep, or hearing, die.

As You Like It

Amiens: Under the greenwood tree
Who loves to lie with me,
And turn his merry note
Unto the sweet bird's throat,
Come hither, come hither, come hither.
Here shall he see
No enemy
But winter and rough weather.

As You Like It

Amiens: Blow, blow, thou winter wind,
Thou art not so unkind
  As man's ingratitude;
Thy tooth is not so keen,
Because thou art not seen,
  Although thy breath be rude.
Heigh-ho! sing heigh-ho! unto the green holly.
Most friendship is feigning, most loving
        mere folly.
  Then, heigh-ho, the holly!
  This life is most jolly.

Freeze, freeze, thou bitter sky,
That dost not bite so nigh
  As benefits forgot;
Though thou the waters warp,
Thy sting is not so sharp
  As friend rememb'red not.
Heigh-ho! *etc.*

— 53 —

As You Like It

Lord: What shall he have that kill'd the deer?
His leather skin and horns to wear.
   Then sing him home.

Take thou no scorn to wear the horn;
It was a crest ere thou wast born.
   Thy father's father wore it;
   And thy father bore it.
The horn, the horn, the lusty horn,
Is not a thing to laugh to scorn.

As You Like It

Pages: It was a lover and his lass,
   With a hey, and a ho, and a hey nonino,
That o'er the green corn-field did pass
   In the spring time, the only pretty ring time,
When birds do sing, hey ding a ding, ding.
Sweet lovers love the spring.

Between the acres of the rye,
   With a hey, and a ho, and a hey nonino,
These pretty country folks would lie,
   In the spring time *etc.*

This carol they began that hour,
   With a hey, and a ho, and a hey nonino,
How that a life was but a flower,
   In the spring time *etc.*

And therefore take the present time,
   With a hey, and a ho, and a hey nonino,
For love is crowned with the prime,
   In the spring time *etc.*

The Two Noble Kinsmen

Boy: Roses, their sharp spines being gone,
Not royal in their smells alone,
   But in their hue;
Maiden pinks, of odour faint,
Daisies smell-less, yet most quaint,
   And sweet thyme true;

Primrose, first-born child of Ver,
Merry springtime's harbinger,
   With harebells dim;
Oxlips, in their cradles growing,
Marigolds, on deathbeds blowing,
   Lark's-heels trim;

All dear nature's children sweet,
Lie fore bride and bridegroom's feet,
   Blessing their sense.
Not an angel of the air,
Bird melodious, or bird fair,
   Is absent hence.

The crow, the sland'rous cuckoo, nor
The boding raven, nor chough hoar,
   Nor chatt'ring pie,
May on our bridehouse perch or sing,
Or with them any discord bring,
   But from it fly.

THE TWO NOBLE KINSMEN

Three Queens: Urns and odours, bring away,
Vapours, sighs, darken the day;
   Our dole more deadly looks than dying.
Balms and gums and heavy cheers,
Sacred vials filled with tears,
   And clamours through the wild air flying:

Come all sad and solemn shows,
That are quick-eyed pleasure's foes.
We convent naught else but woes,
We convent naught else but woes.

Index of First Lines

NOTES

WILLIAM SHAKESPEARE'S working life probably spanned no more than twenty years, but in that time he wrote, or had a hand in writing, thirty-eight plays as well as several books of poems.

The Two Noble Kinsmen, a tragi-comedy first published in 1634, was probably written in collaboration with John Fletcher (1579-1625). There is also evidence that Shakespeare collaborated with the same dramatist on *Henry the Eighth*, published in 1623 as *The Famous History of the Life of King Henry the Eighth*, but known to its first audiences as *All Is True*.